Victor Langlois

Description of the Armenian Monastery on the Island of St. Lazarus-Venice

Followed by a Compendium of the History and Literature of Armenia from the French

Victor Langlois

Description of the Armenian Monastery on the Island of St. Lazarus-Venice
Followed by a Compendium of the History and Literature of Armenia from the French

ISBN/EAN: 9783744727112

Printed in Europe, USA, Canada, Australia, Japan

Cover: Foto ©ninafisch / pixelio.de

More available books at **www.hansebooks.com**

DESCRIPTION

OF THE ARMENIAN MONASTERY

ON THE ISLAND

OF ST. LAZARUS-VENICE

FOLLOWED

BY A COMPENDIUM OF THE HISTORY

AND LITERATURE OF ARMENIA

FROM THE FRENCH
OF

VICTOR LANGLOIS

LATE MEMBER OF THE ARMENIAN ACADEMY OF ST. LAZARUS OF
VENICE, OF THE ACADEMY OF SCIENCE AT TURIN,
KNIGHT OF THE ROYAL RELIGIOUS AND MILITARY ORDER OF
SAINT MAURICE AND SAINT LAZARUS

VENICE

TYPOGRAPHY OF ST. LAZARUS

1874

PREFACE

BY

THE TRANSLATOR

In placing before the Public the English edition of the original work, entitled; "Notice sur le Couvent Arménien de l'île Saint-Lazare de Venise„, etc., I take pleasure in announcing that, its translation has been solicited of me by the good Father James D^r. Issaverdenz, Member of the well known monastic Order, which bears the name of its founder, "Mekhithar„, with whom some of my readers may already be acquainted. The very noble and worthy object of this Order (or Society) is, the propagation of knowledge and enlightenment among their Eastern Brethren, of which the present work gives ample proof and information.

I need hardly refer to works of either ancient or modern writers, in which the interest, — so general for Armenian affairs and especially those of the "Mekhitharists„ — has been widely exhibited, since they are well known to friends of Oriental Literature; among the recent American publications I may mention M^r. Howell's work, entitled: "Venetian Life„ in which he gives a very interesting account of "The Armenians„; that of Mrs. H. H. called: "Bits of Travel„ in which the description of "The Convent of San Lazzaro„ etc. etc. will, no doubt, be read with interest.

In conclusion I sincerely hope, that my humble contribution to the Armenian Publishing-Institute of "San Lazzaro„ through the present translation, (to which — I beg to add — the kind services rendered me by an esteemed American Lady, deserve due claim), may be succeeded by others of greater merit and extent, and that the pages of this little work may be perused with as much pleasure as I have experienced in translating them.

FREDERICK SCHRÖDER

New York, January, 1874.

DESCRIPTION

OF THE ARMENIAN MONASTERY

ON THE ISLAND

OF ST. LAZARUS-VENICE

FIRST PART

History of Mekhithar; The Mekhitharist Congregation, and a description of the Isle of St. Lazarus.

The Monastery of the Armenians of Venice is situated in the Isle of Saint Lazarus, (San Lazzaro) a quarter of a league from the "Little Square ,, (Piazzetta) from which, near the Palace of Doges, rise the two columns which support the statue of St. Theodore, and the winged Lion of St. Mark, the Evangelist.

After passing Point Giudecca and entering the Lagoon, one beholds the Isle of St. Lazarus and the square belfry of the Monastery surmounted by a dome, rising with all the elegance and majesty of a Minaret between the Monastery of San Servolo and the old Lazzeretto, which are situated on adjacent Islets, separated by a branch of the Orfano Canal.

As soon as the elegant and swift Gondola which transports visitors, has cleared the Cape formed by the angle of the Isle, one sees St. Lazarus, which, with its brick-coloured buildings and its tufts of verdure resembles an Oasis in the Desert.

In this abode of peace, piety and science, an Armenian Colony has established itself, and there reside the Monks of the community, standing, one may say, in Europe and looking toward the East — the cradle of the Armenian race.

The Isle of St. Lazarus is mentioned for the first time in the Venetian Archives in the 12th. century. At this epoch Hubert, Abbot of St. Hilarion, conveyed by a deed or charter this then wild desert land to the Seigneur Leone Paolini, a personage celebrated for his many virtues.

In 1182 the Republic of Venice bought this Islet from Paolini and made it an Asylum or Hospital for Lepers arriving from the East; (hence the name St. Lazarus who was considered the Patron of those afflicted with the Pest), and numerous, indeed, were the victims of that scourge, which, in ancient times and during the Middle-ages, desolated the Occident as well as the Orient.

When Leprosy had to a great extent disappeared from the most frequented parts of Asia and Africa, the Isle was abandoned, and after the lapse of ages, there remained but a few crumbling ruins, half concealed among the trees beneath whose shade the poor Fishermen of the Adriatic built their miserable huts.

Five centuries latter — April 1715 — there was an arrival in Venice of twelve Monks, who had been for some time established in the Morea, but had at length been compelled to flee on account of the invasion of that country by the Turks. Their chief bore the name of Mekhithar, which in the Armenian language signifies *Consoler*; he was born in Sivas — anciently Sebaste —, in Asia Minor, and was the only child of Peter and Sharistan, Armenians of that city; he was baptized by the name of " Manoug ,, resembling in his country's idiom the name " Infant Jesus ,,.

At an early age Mekhithar exhibited proofs of a superior mind; being endowed with quickness of perception, and rare intelligence, he made rapid progress in his studies, first under the direction of two nuns, and afterwards under the supervision of the Monks of Garmir-Vank (the Red Convent), to whose care his education had been committed. At the age of 15 he received from the Bishop Ananias the Monk's habit, the name of "Mekhithar„ and the title of Deacon.

At 20 Mekhithar was ordained a Priest, and traversed Asia, preaching the Gospel to his fellow-men, teaching theology, and endeavouring to re-unite in the great communion of the Roman Church, the different sects that ignorance of true principles, and misunderstandings of certain matters had raised up among the Armenians. Mekhithar, longing to diffuse the light of Faith, and the benefits of Science among his fellow-men, undertook long and perilous journeys; he visited first Etchmiadzin, a vast Monastery built on the site of Vagharshabad, (the ancient capital of Armenia), which is used to-day as the residence of the Supreme or High Patriarch (Catholicos) of the Armenian dissenters; then he returned to his own country Sebaste and afterward went to the Monastery of Passen, where the Bishop confided to his care the Church, and instruction of the young people. Very soon afterward Mekhithar undertook new journeys, and this time he reached Syria and stopped at Aleppo, where, influenced by the suggestions of a French Missionary — the Jesuit Antoine Beauvilliers, he decided to visit Rome. Provided by this Jesuit Father with a letter of recommendation, he embarked for the Isle of Cyprus, where he became so seriously ill, that he was forced to abandon his project. As soon as Mekhithar became convalescent, he returned to Sivas to recuperate his health and passed some time in the Convent

"Sourp Nishan„ (Holy Cross), where he was ordained "Vartabied„ (Doctor). Comprehending fully the grave responsibilities which this new title imposed upon him, he undertook new journeys to Asia Minor and also visited Constantinople, preaching everywhere the truths of the Catholic faith.

Unforeseen circumstances obliged Mekhithar to leave Constantinople, and he returned to his country, deferring to a future day his evangelical labours in distant lands.

Having re-entered the Convent of Passen, Mekhithar displayed extraordinary zeal in his theological labours and gave proofs of ardent devotion and piety by his conduct during a fearful epidemic which desolated the country. Subsequently, when the Plague had ceased its ravages, Mekhithar left Sivas to return to the Capital of the Sultans, and there spread abroad the light of the true faith. In 1700 he arrived in Constantinople and there preached union, among his co-religionists, submission to the Church of Rome, and the Christian faith, which would preserve and maintain a spirit of Nationality. The Missionary Priest now retired with three of his disciples to Pera, and there conceived the design of founding a Monastic association, for the purpose of imparting to his countrymen instruction so necessary to the well being of the people, and to the propagation of that christian faith which enables us to bear the trials of life. It was at Pera that Mekhithar published the first prayer-book and those educational works, which inaugurated the printing establishment of the Mekhitharists. The principal work of the Armenian press at Pera was, " The Imitation of Jesus Christ„. Nevertheless jealousy caused perfidious attacks upon Mekhithar, who, incapable of struggling alone, and expecting no support against a powerful party, was at first obliged to seek refuge among the Capuchin Fathers, and finally claim the protection of the French Ambassador.

A longer sojourn in Constantinople being utterly impracticable, Mekhithar resolved to seek elsewhere that safety and tranquillity so necessary to the labours of the increasing congregation; he therefore made arrangements to depart with his pupils for the Morea, a Christian country, then under the sway of the Venetians. Mekhithar assembled his disciples, imparted to them his intention of leaving Turkey, and deeming it imprudent for the Community to depart in a body, thereby attracting the attention of enemies, he proposed to divide his companions into groups. The rendez-vous was to be the city of Modon, on the ramparts of which floated the standard of St. Mark.

Prior to separating from his companions Mekhithar exhorted them not to lose courage, and placing himself with them under the protection of the Mother of God, he gave them, as a rallying-word, the titles of " Adopted Children of Mary „ and "Doctors of Penitence „. These appellations became thenceforward the device or motto of the Congregation, and had reference to their consecration, and to the persecutions they had endured for the true faith [1].

Some of the Monks journied to Morea in advance of the Community, in order

---

[1] The Arms of the religious Order of the Mekhitharists are represented by a Cross, surrounded by four cantons of the emblems of St. Anthony: « the Flame, the Bell, the Gospel, and the Staff „. On each of the branches of the Cross one reads a letter, Ո. Կ. Կ̇. Ս., initials of the four following words: « Adopted sons of the Virgin, Doctors of Penitence „.

to survey the country and select an establishment; shortly afterward Mekhithar and his companions, who had experienced innumerable difficulties, arrived in Modon. The refugees were welcomed with marked favour, and although the Priest and all who accompanied him, were considered subjects of the Porte, they were above all, Christians, and therefore an honorable hospitality was accorded to them.

Immediately after his installation in Modon, Mekhithar's first care was to subject his Community to fixed rules, and then to build a Church and a Convent. Pope Clement XI. confirmed the existence of the new order, approved its constitution, suggesting the rule of St. Benoit, which was substituted for that of St. Augustin that had at first been chosen, and acknowledging as Abbot him, who for long years had given to the Catholic faith such earnest proofs of his zeal, his self abnegation and virtues.

To the new Community the future appeared bright and promised repose. In fact for 12 years it prospered and increased; but again God severely tried the faith and patience of Mekhithar and his fellow-workers. The Turks invaded the Morea, and the Venetians being unable to defend Modon, the Convent of the Armenians was pillaged and burned, and the poor Monks left without shelter or earthly resource ; then placed their confidence alone in Her, whom they had chosen as their Patroness. The Venetian Admiral Mocenigo, and the Governor of the Morea, Angelo Emo, sympathizing deeply with the fearful distress of the unfortunate Community, yielded to their earnest entreaties for permission to embark on a government vessel which was about to leave for Venice.

In the month of April, 1715, a boat just detached from a galley, bearing the standard of St. Mark, reached the Sclavonic Quay; this bark carried Mekhithar and his companions, seeking the hospitality of Venice, and anxious to shelter themselves under the wings of the Lion of the Adriatic.

The powerful Republic accorded to the oppressed fugitives a welcome worthy the grandeur of Venice, and on the 8th. of September 1717, the Senate ceded to Mekhithar and his Community, the Isle of St. Lazarus for ever. The Law did not at that time permit the establishments of any new Communities within the limits of the city.

The Armenian Monks at once hastened to occupy the ruins on the Island, formerly assigned to the lepers, and the Abbot ordered the most necessary repairs to be at once made on the crumbling and dilapidated buildings which still remained.

While the Monks were employed in the construction of dwellings, the Abbot established certain rules for the Government of the Community, and made arrangements to carry out the moral, religious and political measures which he designed to effect; his object was the regeneration of the Armenian people.

The Abbot impressed upon the association the fact, that time and patience would be requisite to accomplish his purposes, and that precipitation would but lead to disorder and ruin.

The Armenian Priests profited by their experiences, their trials and adversities, and the result is, that in the course of a century their Convent has become the intellectual centre of a Nation, the guiding Star of old Armenia, leading its people into the paths of civilization.

The care given to the construction of the divers edifices which composed the Monastery, did not prevent Mekhithar from attending to the intellectual improvement of the Association, and particular attention was paid to the Novices who come each year to increase the establishment.

Throughout his entire life the Abbot was a model of industry, and devoted every leisure moment to study. Translations of moral, religious and scientific works were accomplished under his able direction, and the printing establishment, which he organized in the Monastery, produced numerous books, that during his life were forwarded to Constantinople, into Asia-Minor, and in fact to every place where Armenians could be reached.

The Monastery was completed in 1740 by the founder himself, as the following Armenian and Latin inscription placed over the door of the Refectory indicates:

ՄԵՆԱՍՏԱՆՍ ԱՅՍ ԸՍՏ ԲՈԼՈՐԻՆ
ՇԻՆՆԱԼ ԵՂԵԻ Ի ՓԱՌՍ ՓՐԿՉԻՆ.
ՑԱՐԲԱՑՈՒԹԵՆՆ ՍԵԲԱՍՏԱՑԻՈՑ
ՄԽԻԹԱՐԱՑ ՎԱՐԴԱՊԵՏԻՆ

FUIT HOC MONASTERIUM TOTUM
TEMPORE MECHITHAR PETRI EX
SEBASTE, I. ABBATIS EXTRUCTUM,
AN. 1740.

A few years after Mekhithar had completed the work he had undertaken, a dangerous disease manifested itself by alarming symptoms. For three years the venerable Abbot bore his physical sufferings with the most angelic patience; all medical skill was powerless, malady was pronounced incurable. Finally the Abbot Mekhithar yielded his soul to God on the 27th. of April 1749, aged 74 years. Prior to his departure the faithful Father committed his colabourers and children to the care of the Omnipotent, and his body was deposited at the foot of the Chief Altar of the Convent Chapel. A simple stone alone marks the spot where the mortal remains of the holy Abbot repose.

From that time the Monks of St. Lazarus took the name of "Mekhitharists„,, in memoriam of the founder of their Community.

Steven Melkon (Melchior) of Constantinople succeeded Mekhithar as Abbot. It was during his administration that some of the Monks, who differed from him in their opinions or views of monastic discipline, left the Isle of St. Lazarus under the leadership of Babik, and founded first at Trieste, and afterward at Vienna, in Austria, an entirely distinct Community, although it bore the same name, and worked for similar objects.

Melkon died in 1800, and was succeeded by Aconce Köwer, born in Transylvania, where an Armenian Colony was settled. His family was noble and he was the first Abbot honoured with the dignity of Archbishop, a title conferred upon him by the Court of Rome. This Prelate lived in troubled times; Bonaparte having conquered Italy and annihilated the Venetian Republic, determined to abolish Monastic Institutions, and that of the Armenians was about to be suppressed, when Providence saved it from this misfortune. Thanks to the nationality of the Monks, and the cultivation of literature and the sciences in their Institutions, the Mekhitharists obtained permission to establish an Academy, a privilege to which they were in reality entitled by their useful and scientific labours.

By these means the wise Aconce was enabled to save the Armenian Monastery from that ruin which overwhelmed all the Convents of Italy, and yet in no wise did he change the Monastic order; thus the Monks of St. Lazarus acquired another title to the gratitude of their compatriots.

After an administration of 24 years, Aconce was replaced by Sukias de Somal, who succeeded to the double title of Abbot and Archbishop in 1824.

Under the direction of Sukias, the Community made great progress. This venerable Prelate gave an impetus to scientific researches and inspired a love for literature. Animated by their Abbot the Monks published remarkable scientific and literary works. At once editions of Armenian classics, (until then neglected and unedited), and translations of the chef-d'oeuvres of foreign writers appeared. This ardor, inspired by Sukias, himself a distinguished writer and critic, has not yet abated. It was also during the administration of Sukias that the National Colleges of Venice and Padua were founded.

In 1846 the venerable Sukias finished his earthly career, and was succeeded by George Hurmuz, the present Abbot-General, who at the time of his installation assumed the title of " Archbishop of Siunic „ , one, which his predecessors had formerly borne.

Although it is customary to eulogize the dead, propriety as well as a respectful friendship obliges us to leave to others the duty of reporting at some future day, the valuable services which have been rendered to the Community by Monseigneur Hurmuz; we limit ourselves to the statement, that the worthy Archbishop of Siunic wears on his breast numerous decorations, testimonies of esteem bestowed by Monarchs. Monseigneur George Hurmuz is a "Commander of the Iron Crown of Austria „; has been invested with " the order of SS. Maurice and Lazarus of Italy„; with those of the " Nishan Ifthikar, „ " Medjidié „ and the " Lion and Sun of Persia „; and he has also been decorated a " Chevalier de l'ordre de la Légion d'honneur „ .

After this explanation of the origin and developement of the Mekhitharist Congregation, let us enter the interior of this simple and elegant abode, a fit asylum for religion and science. It seems like a waif detached from the Ark of the Covenant, and impelled to the bright shores of Italy by the will of the Omnipotent.

II.

As soon as the iron prow of the Gondola touches the marble stairs which are laved by the clear waters of the Lagoon, the door of the Monastery opens as if by enchantment, and the Visitor passes into the Atrium which is adorned with flowers and shrubs. Immediately one encounter a Father of the Order, clad in the black robe of the Eastern Monks, and having encircled his waist by a leather belt. He is the guide whose duty it is to conduct the Visitor through the Establishment, and exhibit to him the chapel, the library, printing-presses, gardens, etc, etc.

The Community consists of about sixty members or " Vartabieds „ and a few " brothers „. We have stated that the Monastery is governed by a General Abbot, who bears the title of Archbishop of Siunie, and that the Prelate who at present exercises these high functions, is Monseigneur George Hurmuz. The Abbot is assisted by a Council of six members, (nominated by the Chapter of the Order), who aid him in the administration of all affairs, temporal and spiritual. The Fathers are occupied with the education of youthful members, the prosecution of scientific and literary researches, the labours of the publishing department and the ordinary duties of a Monastery. The products of their printing-presses form one of the principal revenues of the Community, and serve not only to defray domestic expenses, but to provide for the education of young men who are admitted as Seminarists. Several of the Fathers of the Armenian Community reside in Venice and some in foreign lands, where they direct educational houses, as at Paris and Constantinople ; or they travel as Missionaries, labouring to carry out the designs of their founder.

On entering this peaceful and secluded abode, the silence of which is only disturbed by the wind sighing among the cypress-trees, and the waves beating on the neighbouring shores, one traverses a garden surrounded by the arcades of the Cloister. Broad stairs lead to the corridors, where, from numerous windows, one beholds delightful views, including the Lido, which bounds the horizon, and seems to form a barrier to the blue waves of the Adriatic.

One first enters the Church which is of Gothic Architecture; passing the peristyle we see two Monuments, that on the right, contains the ashes of Constantine Zuchola, who was a Curator of the Hospital, before the Island came into the possession of the Mekhitarists; the inscription on the monument is:

HOC PROBUS ET SAPIENS ORTUS DE PROLE ZUCHOLA CLAUDITUR IN TUMULO, CUI CONSTANTINUS IN URBE NOMEN ERAT, LAZARI CURATOR, AMATOR, ET ALMI COMPATIENS INOPUM, DOMINE IN HONORE SUPERNI.

The white marble monument on the left is quite modern; it was reared by the Chevalier Alexander Rafael, an Armenian of the East Indies, eldest son of Edward Rafael, patron of the college which bears his name, and was established in Venice in the ancient Palace Zenobio, situated in the quarter " dei Carmini ,,.

On each side of the exterior door are inscriptions in the Latin and Armenian languages recording the visit of Pope Pius VII. to the Armenian Monastery in 1800.

The Church of Mekhithar was rebuilt or remodeled from the remains of one which had occupied the site nearly six centuries prior to the advent of the Armenian Community; Mekhithar changed the low flat ceiling into a vaulted roof, and replaced the stone pillars by columns of red marble.

The Church of St. Lazarus is not at all remarkable for its architectural beauty, and is certainly eclipsed by the magnificence of St. Mark's, and those of S.S. John and Paul, and the

Salute, as well as by other marvels of Art that Venice contains. Nevertheless, to one who has been dazzled by the art-treasures of the Queen of the Adriatic, the simplicity of the chapel of the Mekhitharists of St. Lazarus is quite refreshing.

The Church contains five altars; at the foot of the high altar, lies (as we have already stated) the tomb of the founder. It is covered by a simple slab, destitute of ornament, and bearing merely an inscription in the Armenian language, commemorative of the life and death of the pious and zealous Mekhithar.

On the right hand a beautiful copy of the Virgin, by Sassoferrato, executed by Jean Emir, a converted Turk, attracts considerable attention.

One of the minor altars is adorned by a picture of Tiridates, the first christian monarch of Armenia, who was baptized by St. Gregory the Illuminator; another is surmounted by a figure of Christ well executed in marble. Among the chief paintings may be mentioned, one of St. Mesrob, the inventor of the Armenian Alphabet, and a translator of the Gospels, and another of St. Isaac, a patriarch of Armenia.

There is an altar dedicated to St. Anthony, the first patron of the Community, and as a matter of course, one to their patroness, the Virgin.

The Sacristy contains many -rich ornaments and some precious vases; the sacerdotal vestments of the founder, and those of the Abbots who have succeeded him, are also preserved there.

Few services are more impressive than the celebration of High Mass in the Armenian Chapel, when the venerable Prelate, surrounded by the Monks and Novices of the community, clad in their sacred habiliments, intones with them the sacred anthems of the old christian Poets of Armenia. One could readily imagine he heard the ancient bards of Koghten reciting, accompanied by the *pampirn*, those sacred ballads, which were so much admired even in the 5th. century, that Moses of Chorene has preserved some of them in his history of Armenia.

One great fête days one may witness all the pomp and splendor of the Armenian service; then the Archbishop, the Deacons and Levites, all clad in rich robes of various shades, embroidered with pearls and silk, (the work of Armenian ladies of Constantinople), officiate with an imposing solemnity.

The chants of the Armenians are monotonous as those of the Orient usually are, and sound strangely to Europeans.

The Mekhitharists preserve their national rites as far as possible, and celebrate them in the Armenian language. During the service, while the vaporous incense half conceals the chancel from the rest of the Church, the officiating Priest with his dalmatica and tiara, (resembling that of a Pontiff), seems as if resting on a cloud. At the elevation of the Host, a curtain falls and conceals the sanctuary, as if to hide from spectators the divine mystery.

The Monks of St. Lazarus attend service in their chapel three times per diem; — at 5 o'clock in the morning, at noon, and at 3 o'clock in the afternoon.

The Mekhitharists officiate also at a Church in Venice, called the " Chapel of the Holy Cross „ , which was built at the expense of the Armenian colony, by the architect Sansovino.

On leaving the Church, we visit the refectory, a large apartment, in which the Monks take their repasts in common. It contains a well executed picture of the Lord's Supper, the work of the Venetian artist Novelli who also ornamented the altar of St. Anthony in the Chapel of the Monastery.

The most interesting part of the house is unquestionably the Library, which is approached by a stairway near the refectory. A vestibule (lighted by a window, which not only opens on the gardens of the Isle, but affords an extended view of the Lido) is used as a Cabinet for curiosities. One Alcove contains some Armenian antiquities, and objects of interest from other countries, among which is a Madonna with the Infant Jesus in her arms; it is of stone, and on the reverse bears the name of the Sculptor, Alexander, an Armenian. There is also a beautifully chased silver drinking-cup which bears an Armenian inscription to the effect that it once belonged to a person named Lazarus.

A particularly striking relic is the antique armor of a warrior and horse discovered in the environs of Erzeroum.

The large apartment containing the 30,000 volumes which form the Library, is well lighted by windows that also open on the gardens. The ceiling is adorned by medallions, one representing the martyrdom of St. Catherine, and the others the most celebrated Divines of the Roman and Armenian Churches.

The books are arranged on shelves, and in elegantly carved cabinets; they are principally on religious and scientific subjects, yet there are some choice editions of rare literary treasures, worthy the attention of the most ardent bibliophile.

In the middle of the Library is a case containing a numismatic collection; some of the coins are extremely ancient, others belong to the Middle-Ages; those of Asia, as well as the medals of Armenia, are especially interesting.

On a stand rests the bust of Mekhithar, it is of Carrara marble and was executed in Rome in 1833 by the Chevalier Fabris, a distinguished pupil of Canova's. A pedestal supports an excellent, though diminutive, statue of Pope Gregory XVI; it was presented by that Pontiff who honoured the Mekhitharists with the title of "Friends„ .

Some Birmese Papyrus is placed in a pendant case, in one corner of the hall; it was bequeathed to the Monastery by M. Lazarowitch, a rich Armenian of India. Opposite the Papyrus is a powerful telescope.

Undoubtedly one of the most curious objects in the Museum is a cedar coffin containing an Egyptian Mummy; this is a present from a celebrated Armenian, Boghos-Bey, who so zealously seconded the efforts of the Viceroy of Egypt to promote civilization.

Over the principal door of the Library hangs a fine sea-view, the work of an Armenian, John Aïwazowsky, a Chevalier of the Order of St. Ann, and of the Legion of Honour, one of the most able artists of Russia.

The Cabinets containing the Manuscripts are in an attic room; these documents, two thousand in number, constitute the intellectual wealth of the Monastery. This collection in the Armenian language, is the most valuable in Europe, yet it is inferior to that of Etchmiadzin in Armenia Proper, (or the Great Armenia).

All the Manuscrips are bound and carfully arranged in glass cabinets; some of them are simply written on parchment, others are adorned with vignettes that have been greatly admired by artists. The Fathers have prepared an accurate catalogue which forms a quarto-volume.

In another apartment the Fathers have placed copies of every Armenian work published abroad, as well as one sample of each book printed in their own Establishment. Over the door of this room hangs a portrait of Napoleon III. presented to the Monastery by the French Government, as a testimony of the esteem France entertains for the Armenian nation, and a token of her appreciation of the labours of the Mekhitharist Community.

The printing establishment of the Monastery merits particular attention; there Italian compositors work under the direction of a Monk to whom is delegated the supervision of the typographical department. From the time of Mekhithar until the present day, the presses of St. Lazarus have produced annually a considerable number of works of various kind; these are despatched to Turkey, Russia, Persia and even to the Indies. The Monks of St. Lazarus have been awarded premiums of the first class for specimens of their skill in the typographic art; viz. at the Expositions universelles de Paris 1855-67; at the World's Fair London in 1862; at the Exhibition in Florence in 1861; and at Vienna 1873.

It was in this establishment that Mekhithar's translation of the Bible was published, also the works of celebrated Mekhitharists, as well as translations from the Greek and Latin classics.

From this prolific press issued too, translations of the best French and Italian books ancient and modern; to it we owe also editions of Armenian classics and the works of Eusebius and Philon the Israelite; the original writings of the latter having been destroyed or lost, there exists to-day alone the Armenian version.

We have already stated that after

the conquest of Italy by Napoleon Bonapart the Mekhitharists founded a national Academy, all the members of which were monks of their Community. This Academy which has increased and flourished, has assumed the duty of editing certain works which are issued annually, and it is designed to compile an Armenian Dictionary on the same principle as that of the Academie Française. Moreover a monthly Journal, called the Polyhistor (Pasmavèb) is published and contains contributions from Members of the Academy abroad as well as within the walls of the Monastery, and the Monks willingly admit to the fraternity learned foreigners, who are willing to devote themselves to study of Armenian literature. Messrs. Brosset, Reinaud, Petermam, etc. etc, are members of the Mekhitharist Academy, and Lord Byron and Sylvester de Sacy formerly belonged to it.

The Monastry recruits its novices from all countries inhabited by Armenians, and each year the fraternity confers the title of "Doctor„ or "Vartabed„ on those young members who have passed a satisfactory examination, and have fully determined to conform to the duties of a cenobitical life.

The course of instruction is divided into three terms or courses; the first is for children up to the age of 17; they are taught the classics (or humanities), modern languages of Europe, mathematics and morality. The second is designed for novices who desire to take orders, and they continue the studies of the first course, by rhetoric, Latin, and the exact sciences. The third term is devoted to philosophy, theology, Greek, etc. etc.

After the final examination which follows the third course, the professed Monks are ordained Priests and assume the title of "Father,,. Then the Abbot assigns to each some duty, but never any menual occupation; it is the lay-brothers, and domestics who perform all the servile labour, such as the duties of cleansing the Monastery, and attending to the cattle, the stables or gardens. After a sojourn of several years in the Monastery, the Fathers are sent out on missions; prior to their departure the Abbot confers upon them the title of "Vartabed,, or "Doctor,, .

Each member of the Community has a private cell. The Abbot lives among the fraternity in a simple suite of rooms consisting of a cell, an oratory and a Parlor; it is in the latter that the Archbishop of Siunic receives distinguished foreigners.

Before we leave this place we must visit the garden, which is embellished with luxuriant vines bearing luscious grapes. In a retired corner of the Isle is a small vineyard that furnishes a white wine which the Monks use for sacramental purposes; they have given it the name at once biblical and national of "wine of Ararat,, .

On fête-days an Ottoman banner, presented to the Community by the Sultan Abd-ul-Medjid, floats from a high mast on the shore of the Island.

The gardens are in excellent order, and from them one may enjoy most enchanting views; in the distance loom up the Julian Alps covered with snow, near by lies Venice with its red spires, white domes, marble palaces and symbolic columns. Then there is the azure sea with black gondolas gliding to and fro, and to the right the Lido, whose verdure is reflected in the Adriatic; to complete the scene and enhance its charms the Lagoon is filled with beautiful little Islands, extending many miles.

At one extremity of the Isle are the stables of the Monastery where fat kine are fed on the rich grass that is daily brought by boat from the Lido.

Behind the choir of the Chapel one finds a grave of Cypress-trees, and a few simple tombs; these are the graves of some unfortunate pilgrims from the Orient, who, despairing of ever again beholding their native land, begged to be laid beneath the shadow of the "vineyard of Ararat,,.

Near the Printing department is an apartment used as a depository for all the literary productions of the Monastery; here visitors are shewn a small volume containing the prayers of St. Nerses in thirty-three languages. Finally the register, in which each visitor is expected to sign his or her name, is presented. It forms a curious collection of autographs; side by side we find the names of kings and distinguished travellers. Each leaf contains a sentiment, a motto or phrase, souvenirs of the numerous visitors from the Monarch down to the humblest traveller. Lord Byron was one of the first who signed the register ; after his autograph follow those of the Emperors and Empresses of Austria, of Western Princes, of Military men whose fame has filled the world, and the names of Poets who have immortalized the beauties of Venice in verse.

One rarely encounters many Fathers in the Monastery, the majority of them are absent on missions to Constantinople, Asia, or France.

The Mekhitharists have two colleges, one in Venice, the other in Paris, which were endowed by private individuals. Two rich Armenians of Madras, bequeathed considerable sums to the Monks of St. Lazarus for the purpose of educating their co-religionists; the revenues from these bequests, support these colleges. That of Venice was founded in 1836 in the Pesaro palace, opposit the palace of the Duchess of Berri; it was afterward removed to the Zenobio palace, and now bears the name of its founder "Rafael,,. Here forty pupils receive a complete education; they are under the supervision of a Mekhitharist Priest, who is assisted by several of his confrères.

The other College was first established in Padua in 1834, but was removed to Paris in 1846, where it now flourishes in a magnificent Hotel, rue de Monsieur, originally built for the Duchess de Bourbon. In this Armenian Institute (endowed by Samuel Moorad), are sixty pupils, under the direction of the Priests of the Mekhitharist Community, who are ably assisted by French professors. Both Colleges have sent forth into the world distinguished scholars who have attained high positions in the military and civil service of Turkey and Armenian-Persia, and many have proved their ability in commerce as well as in different departments of the arts and sciences.

In the second part we will give an epitome of the history of Armenia, and some details respecting its geographical position. We will also consecrate a few pages in explanation of the invaluable services which the Mekhitharists have rendered to Armenian literature, and will give some information regarding the recent journeys made to Asiatic countries once possessed by the Armenians, and where even now they are numerous.

SECOND PART

History of Armenia, and Armenian literature from ancient times down to the present time.

I.

The vast country called Armenia, or Armenia Major, occupies all that region of Asia situated between the southern boundary of the Caucassian Mountains and Mesopotamia; and extends from the Euphrates river to the Caspian Sea, which forms its eastern boundary. The centre of this immense circle is Mount Ararat on which, according to Biblical tradition, Noah's Ark rested after the deluge; around this circle are Mingrelia, Imerethia, Gouria, Georgia, Kakhet, Shirwan, Talish, Aderbeidjan and Kurdistan.

Armenia Minor extends into Asia Minor like a peninsular; it lies partially between the Mountains of Amanus and the Black Sea, and is bounded on the east by Armenia Major, and on the south by Cilicia and Syria. Cilicia, which for three centuries was the seat of an Armenian Kingdom, is separated from Armenia Minor, by the Taurus Mountains; this province is entirely surrounded by mountains except on the South, where it is bounded by the Mediterranean Sea.

Armenian Geographers divide Armenia Major into fifteen provinces, which are subdivided into cantons and districts. These provinces are Upper Armenia, Daïk, Koukark, Oudi, Fourth Armenia, Dourouperan, Aghdznik, Ararat, Vasbouragan, Sunia, Artzakh, Païdagaran, Mogk, Gordjaïk and Persian Armenia. The country termed Armenia Minor comprises First, Second and Third Armenia under the dominion of the Greeks.

The present division is very different; the Turks who possess all Armenia Minor, and the countries on both sides of Euphrates, as well as those south of the Mountains of Georgia and adjoining Mesopotamia, have divided this immense territory into Pashalics, the principal cities of which are Erzeroom, Kars, Bayazid, Van and Diarbeker.

During the past and present centuries, the Russians have wrested from the Persians a considerable portion of Armenia Major; they now possess the countries situated between the rivers Kour (Cyrus) and Araxes. They also hold the cities of Erevan, Nakhitchevan, Asdabad, Chaki, Shirwan, Shamakhi, Berdé, and the Monastery of Etchmiadzin. Moreover the Russians have also conquered the countries situated south of Ararat, a part of Vasbouragan and the country lying between the confluent of the Araxes river and the Caspian Sea. To the Persians, (who one century ago, occupied the greater part of Armenia) there remain only the countries situated between the Turkish possessions, the Mountains of Kurdistan and Lake Ormiah.

History has preserved accounts of some of the ancient cities of Armenia, and to this day the ruins of several of them still exist. Among the most remarkable are Garin or Theodosiopolis, (now Erzeroom), Ani, (the ancient capital of the Bagratides), the ruins of which still excite the wonder and admiration of travellers, Vagharshabad, (on the ruins of which stands the Monastery of Etchmiadzin), Van, Ourha or Edessa, (the capital of the Abgars), Medzpine or Nisibe and Erevan.

From traditions preserved in the works of Armenian writers we learn that the country called by Europeans " Armenia „ and by the inhabitants "Haïasdan „ or country of Haïk, was founded by the patriarch Haïk who was the son of Torgomah, son of Tiras, son of Gomer, son of Japheth, who was the son of Noah.

Haïk went from Babylon with a colony and settled in the vicinity of Ararat, where he found some inhabitants whom he forced to submit to his authority. Soon afterwards he increased his domain and triumphed over Bel the Nimrod of the Bible.

The successors of Haïk extended the limits of their country, but at length Armenia became tributary to the Assyrians and was considered by them a mere Satrapy; it ramained subject to Nineveh until the reign of Barouir who raised the standard of revolt against foreign tyrants and achieved independence.

One of the successors of Barouir Tigranes, whom the Armenians call Dikran, greatly enhanced the power of Armenia; but finally, after an existence of nearly 2000 years, the kingdom succumbed to the power of Alexander the Great.

When the powerful Macedonian King undertook the conquest of the old Asiatic World, Armenia, which at that time was governed by a feeble and impotent Prince, was forced to yield to the irresistible power of the Greeks; and when Alexander, anticipating his death, divided his Empire among his successors and Generals, Armenia was bequeathed to the Seleucidae who governed it until the Parthians appeared, conquered the Syrians and established themselves as Masters over a great portion of the domains of the Seleucidae.

The Greek Kings had then held Armenia for one hundred and eighty years.

One of the Parthian Monarchs made a gift of Armenia to his brother Valarsace or Vagharshag, and conferred upon him the title of "King „. The Parthian Prince being deeply interested in his adopted country, increased its importance by brilliant victories, and then secured for it the benefits of a permanent peace. He reorganized the Government, appointed Satraps to rule the distant provinces, (according the usual plan of Oriental Monarchies), and governed all his domains judiciously.

Valarsace was the founder of the Arsacidae dynasty which ruled Armenia for several centuries; finally the country was conquered by the Romans and Persians.

In their first struggles with the Romans, the Armenians gained glorious victories; then for the first time did the Roman Legions, yield the palm of victory to those whom they considered " Asiatic barbarians „.

Tigranes, (Dikran II.) who sustained so nobly the title of " King of Kings „, checked the incursions of his country's foes; but after a few years of success, the Romans conquered, and Anthony avenged the defeats of Gabinius, Crassus, Silus and Ventidius, and Armenia was at last brought under the domination of the Roman Triumvirate.

A new Era now dawned upon the Earth; Christ was born, and His doctrines spreading over the Pagan World, changed the status of humanity.

The seat of the Armenian Government was removed to Edessa (Ourha), where King Abgar, a representative of the Arsacidae, resided. Armenian Historians affirm that he was the first king who embraced the Christian faith.

While one branch of the Arsacidae remained in Osrhoene, the direct descendants of Arsaces managed to sustain themselves in Armenia, despite the opposition and persecution they endured. One of the Kings of this dynasty, Tiridates (or Dertad, son of Chosroes or Khosrow), after having revived to a great extent the glory of his kingdom, embraced Christianity. This Monarch was converted by the eloquence of the Patriarch Gregory (the Illuminator) whom he had at first persecuted.

For a time Armenia exercised some power in Asia, and the new faith triumphed. Kings, Nobles, Patriarchs and the Clergy vied with each other in their endeavours to establish the new Church on a firm basis, and from the Episcopacy came eminent professors of the faith, to fill the pulpit of St. Gregory and spread abroad by their writings those evangelical truths calculated to convert people still absorbed in idolatry, Monotheism and Polytheism.

Armenia had already made considerable progress under the successors of Tiridates and St. Gregory, when the Persians invaded the country and undertook to oppose the doctrines of Zoroaster to the tenets of Christianity.

Diran, King of Armenia, too feeble to resist the Persians, consented to pay the tribute which they exacted, and even accepted the images of Julian, which he caused to be placed in the Churches.

Arsaces II. succeeded Diran: during his reign the Persians triumphed over the Armenians completely, and so thoroughly crushed them, that the king and his posterity became vassals of the Sassanidae. The kingdom of Armenia at first divided between the Romans and Sassanidae, was at last stricken from the roll of Nations, and foreign Governors occupied the land as representatives of the king of Persia and the Emperor of Constantinople.

Had not God signally protected the Christians of Armenia, their nationality would have been totally destroyed; but at this epoch the Omnipotent inspired an obscure Priest, Mesrob, (a disciple of St. Nerses), to endow the Nation with an Alphabet [1], and it is to this great means of disseminating knowledge and the principles of Christianity, that the race of Haïg owes its perpetuation.

Although the Persians had devastated Armenia, and overthrown the Arsacidae, who had reigned for about 500 years, the national spirit was not enti-

---

[1] Mesrob Mashdots, born about the year 360 at Hatsegatz-Avan, in the province of Daron, the most celebrated man in the history of his country; the innumerable services rendered by this great benefactor may be consulted in Curzon's " Armenia,, the Church and Hierarchy.

rely crushed, and at times the Armenians rebelled and made strenuous efforts to resist the conquerors, who endeavored to force upon them Fire worship and the laws of Zoroaster. Some of the attempts at revolt were crowned with success, and, for a short period, the Armenians under Vartan the Mamigonian re-established their nationality and religion. However, the heroes and patriots were unable to resist their enemies, and at length Armenia fell under the yoke of the oppressor. The Persian Governors reduced the Christians to extreme misery. Martyrdom at length crowned these Armenian heroes; such in fact was the barbarous cruelty of the Persians, that the Christians implored death at the hands of their conquerors as a relief from torture and persecution.

The Greeks of Byzantium determined to fly to the rescue of captive and expiring Armenia. Justinian and his successors made several expeditions against the Persians, and Armenia might possibly have regained her freedom, had not enemies even more formidable than the Macedonians, Romans and Persians, suddenly appeared upon the scene, and wrested the country from its oppressors only to place it in a still more odious bondage. These were the Arabs, who had decided to attempt the conquest of the Eastern World in the name of Allah and Mahomet his prophet.

Until the Osdigans, (who succeeded the Persian Marzbans, and the Byzantine Curopalates), ceased to govern that portion of Armenia which was a dependancy of Ottoman Empire, the country was for nearly 500 years tributary to neighbouring conquerors, or else, under the yoke of the Mahomedans. Nevertheless, during the 9th. century the Caliphs re-established a portion of the ancient empire of the Arsacidae on Prince Ashod, a scion of the family of Bagratidae. The capital of this kingdom was Ani, where, for nearly 200 years the dynasty of Ashod continued to reign, but finally they were deposed, and the kingdom fell into the power of the Greeks of Constantinople. Under pretence of a cession of certain territory, Kakig, the last sovereign of this dynasty, made a gift of his kingdom to the Greeks, who subsequently proved traitorous and caused him to be assassinated. Armenia subjugated again, then relapsed into anarchy; the inhabitants groaning under their oppressive yoke, endeavored to revolt; but failing in all efforts to redress their grievances, they determined to emigrate far from their native land.

By the time the Armenian emigrants had reached Taurus and settled on the plains of Cylicia, an extraordinary excitement began to convulse all christian

Europe; it was the impulse to wrest the tomb of Christ from the Infidels. Then the Occident took up arms and marched to attack the Orient.

The Armenians had for some time been settled in Cylicia, when the first Christian armies appeared in Asia-Minor en route to Syria. They had established an independant Government under an Armenian Prince, Roupen the first of the dynasty that occupied the throne of Cylicia at the time of the Crusades; it was the assistance of the Armenians and the protection of their Princes that enabled the Crusaders to reach Antioch so readily.

By way of recompensing the Armenians for services rendered the Crusaders, the Pope and the Emperor of Germany, raised their Prince Léon to the dignity of a Sovereign, and granted to him and his successors the title of " King „.

When the ardor of the Crusaders had abated, the Armenians being deprived of the assistance of Western Christians, were unable to resist the encroachments of the Mussulmen. The sovereigns of the Lusignan dynasty were driven from the throne, and the last Armenian king, Leon VI. of the family de Lusignan, who was for some time imprisoned by the Mamelouks of Egypt, went to France, where he died in 1393 [1].

[1] His body was carried to the tomb clothed in royal robes of white, according to the custom of Armenia, with an open crown upon his head and a golden sceptre in his hand. He lay in state upon an open bier hung with white, and surrounded by the officers of his household, clothed all of them in white robes. He was burried at Paris by the high altar of the church of the Celestines, where his effigy was to be seen upon a black marble tomb under an archway in the wall, and on the tomb was written:

«Cy gist le tres noble et tres excellent Prince, Lyon de Lusignan, quint Roi Latin du

From that date the Armenian kingdom was never reconstituted - king Leo VI the last of this royal line, having left no successor -. The Empire founded by Haïg fell into the power of the Turks, but a great portion of it has during the past century been conquered and appropriated by the Russians.

II.

Very little of the literature of Ancient Armenia is now extant; merely fragments which have been preserved in the annals of the early Christian writers. Not even the names of the ancient Bards of the nation have been chronicled.

Tradition pretends that the nation-

Royaulme d'Armenie, qui rendit l'ame a Dieu a Paris le XXIX. jour de Novembre, l'an de Grace MCCCXCIII." This tomb afterwards was transferred to St. Denis.

al literature was in a flourishing condition long before the Christian era, and writers of the 1st. century cite the names of archaic autors of Armenia. Nevertheless, the persons to whom the early chronicles are attributed, were doubtless foreigners, because their names indicate Persian, Syrian and Greek origin; for example, Mar-Apas Catina, Olympius,Ardites, Khorohbut, etc., which are evidently not Armenian appellations.

The first writers whose works have come down to us in the Armenian language, date only from the 4th. century A. D.

The earliest of these works are those of St. Gregory, the Illuminator, the first Patriarch of Armenia, who composed a great number of homilies, hymns and prayers that have been adopted into the Armenian Church service. Then follow those of Agathange, secretary of King Tiridates, a Grecian, who wrote in his own language a history of the reigning Monarch, and a biography of St. Gregory. These works were subsequently translated into the Armenian tongue. There are several editions of these important books and excellent translations of them in Italian.[1]

St. James of Nisibe, author of dogmatical and moral homilies.[2]

Zenob of Clag [3] historian of the province of Daron.

St. Nerses the Great, author of several ascetic works.

Faustus of Byzantium,[4] who in his national history combines that of Agathange and continues it to A. D. 390.

---

1 Armenian translation published at Constantinople, 1719, 1824. - At Venice, in 1833, 1862; and an Italian translation in 1843.

2 Rome, Armenian text, with a latin translation, 1756. - Venice, 1765. – Constantinople, only text, 1824.

3 Constantinople, 1719. – Venice, 1832.

4 Constantinople, 1730. – Venice, 1832.

St. Isaac the Great, Patriarch of Armenia, who translated the old Testament with so much purity, fidelity and elegance, following the Septuagint or Greek version. Mesrob, surnamed Mashdotz, to whom we are indebted not only for the invention of the present Armenian Alphabet, but for a translation of the New Testament (from the Greek) and the Armenian Euchology. [1]

Isaac and Mesrob were the first to arrange systematically the Armenian Breviary, the hymns, the ritual, the calendar and the liturgy.

The 5th. century, which is the second golden age of Armenian literature, had been prepared by the preceding era. Mesrob, inspired by heaven, had invented the 38 Armenian characters, (written from left to right), which were destined to revolutionize the existing

1 Venice, 1837.

state of science and literature. All the works which had originally een written in Persian, Syriac or Greek characters, were copied in the newly invented Armenian letters, which were also used to translate the Scriptures. Schools were established throughout the country, and the sciences hitherto principally taught in Athens, Alexandria and Rome, began to be zealously pursued here, and these literary and scientific efforts of the people were fostered and encouraged by Vramshabouh, King of Armenia.

The 5th. century produced Eznig, whose principal work is interesting on account of its referene to the various forms of worship among the Ancients. It is moreover a refutation [1] of the creeds of the Persian Fire-worshippers and other Pagans, as well as of the

[1] Venice, 1824, 1849. – French translation at Paris, 1855.

doctrines of the Greek Philosophers, and those of the Marcionites and the Manicheans.

Moses of Chorene, the Father of Armenian Historians, was the author of a History of Armenia, [1] from the beginning of the World down to the destruction of the Arshagounis. This history is particularly useful on account of its frequent and general reference to the Assyrians, Persians, Romans and the Greeks of the lower Empire.

Moses of Chorene composed also a grammar and a treatise on rhetoric, [2] which contains the only passages now extant of the Tragedy of the Peliades, of Euripides; moreover he compiled a

---

1 Amsterdam, 1695. – London, text with latin translation, 1736. – Venice, only text, 1827; text and a french translation, 1841; italian translation, without text, 1841, 1849.

2 Venice, 1796; complete works, 1843 and 1868.

Geography and wrote a number of homilies and sublime hymns.

Mambré, surnamed Verdzanogh (Anagnoste), brother of Moses of Chorene, author of several homilies [1] and a History which is no longer extant.

David, called the "Philosopher„, because he was celebrated in Philosophy, and also translated the philosophical works of Aristotle. [2]

Kewd, a Patriarch of Armenia, a disciple and fellow-worker of Mesrob's.

Johan Mantagouni, also a Patriarch and author of homilies and prayers. [3]

Elisha, who wrote a "History of the Vartanians, „ [4] in which he ably recounts the persecutions the Persians in-

---

[1] Venice, 1833.
[2] Venice, 1833.
[3] Venice, 1836, 1857. –
[4] Constantinople, 1764, 1825. – Russia, 1787. – Venice, 1832, 1842, etc. – the italian translation in 1841. – Paris, 1846, a french translation.

flicted on the Armenians, and the combats sustained by these Christians and the Georgians in defence of their country and religious faith. We owe to Elisha also numerous ascetic works and homilies.[1]

Lazarus Parbetzi,[2] a historian who recorded the invention of the Armenian Alphabet or written characters, the progress of literature, and the various wars of the Armenians against the Persians, their persecutors down to 485, A. D. Parbetzi also translated the Bible.

Years of abundance are often followed by seasons of sterility; this was the case with the literature of Armenia during the 6th. century. Political troubles, and incessant wars under the Persian tyrant Hazguerd, prevented all communication between the Greeks and Armenians. This century is only remark-

1 Complete works, Venice, 1833, 1859. —
2 Venice, 1793, 1872.

able for the regulation of the Calendar,[1] which was agreed upon in a Synod held at Twene in 552, under the Patriarch Moses II, Elevardetzi.

During the 6th. century lived: Abraham, a learned Bishop, who wrote a treatise on the Council of Ephesus, held in 431.

Peter, Archbishop of Sunik, author of different writings and homilies. Abraham and Cyrion, Patriarchs and authors of various ecclesiastical letters.

Even in the following century, lit-

---

[1] The first day of the first year of the new Era commenced on the 11th. of July 552 A. D. By the suppression of one day in leap-years – the years of the Armenians being all uniform – the result was one less in the Armenian Calendar at the end of a space of time, which elapsed between 552 A. D. and 1320, making the difference between the latin and armenian Calendars only 551 years; thus, the year of our Lord 1862 corresponds with that of 1312 of the Armenian era.

erature suffered from the unsettled condition of the Nation. The following writers of that age are some of the most distinguished.

The Patriarch Gomidas, who composed some beautiful hymns to Saint - Hripsimé.[1]

John Mamigonian, author of a History of Daron to the year 640.[2]

Annanias Shiragatzi, author of treatises on Astronomy, weights and measures, Calculus and general mathematics.

Moses Galgantouatzi, author of a History of the Aghouank, (Albanians).[3]

The 8th. century produced but few writers of any note; we may mention three: John IV. Otznetzi, Patriarch of all Armenia, surnamed "The Philos-

[1] Translated into Italian by L. Carrer, Venice. 1842.
[2] Constantinople, 1719. - Venice 1831.
[3] Paris, 1857.

opher„. Of his writings we have a dissertation on the Paulicians, an explanation of the Armenian church service, a collection of the canons of ancient councils, [1] and a number of hymns.

Stephen, Archbishop of Sunik, is best known in the Armenian church as the author of some beautiful hymns, which he composed in honor of the resurrection of Jesus-Christ. He also translated several works from the Greek.

Leo Yeretz, author of an abridged History - written in an elegant and pure style - of the Empire established by Mahomet and maintained by the Caliphs his successors. [2]

The peace which Armenia enjoyed

---

[1] Venice, 1807, 1816, 1834, text with the latin translation, and numerous theological and philological notes.

[2] Translated into French by M. Shahnazarian. Paris, 1856. The Armenian text has been published by the same.

under the wise government of the Pacradouni Princes, exercised a happy influence upon literature; several eminent writers grace this era, but in this limited sketch we can only mention:

Zachariah, a Patriarch, author of some homilies, canticles and ecclesiastical letters.

John IV. a Patriarch, author of a celebrated National History, [1] which is a compilation of the Histories of Moses of Chorene, and the works of Elisha, Corion, Shabouh and latter writers. This History includes a chronicle of the Armenian Patriarchs from the time of St. Gregory to that of the Author. It is written with much care and elegance.

Thomas Ardzruni, [2] author of a History which extends from the time

---

1 Jerusalem, 1843. Translated into French by M. Saint-Martin, and published by Lajard at Paris, 1844.
2 Constantinople, 1852.

of the immediate descendants of Noah down to A. D. 936. Although this history is devoted especially to the glory of Ardzrouni, it contains also records of national events that are considered perfectly authentic.

The cultivation of literature was continued through the 10th. century; among the numerous writers we may mention:

Samuel Gamertchatzoretzi, who composed several articles on ecclesiastical services and ceremonies.

Mesrob Yeretz, who wrote a History of St. Nerses the Great. [1]

Gregory Naregatzi, [2] an elegant and sublime poet, the Pindar of the Armenians. His sacred elegies, (95 in number), are perfect gems of the poetic art, elevated in style and pure in sentiment.

---

1 Madras, 1775; with a history of the Orbelians. – Venice, 1853.
2 Complete works, Venice, 1827, 1840, etc.

Of the numerous editions of these poems, the best is undoubtedly that of Father Gabriel Avedikian. We may also mention his Panegyrics on "The Holy Cross,, "The Virgin, ,, on "the Apostles,, and "St. James of Nisibe,, as well as the canticles and melodies still chanted in the Armenian Church. [1]

Stephen Assolik, author of a History of Armenia from the origin of the Nation to the year of our Lord 1004. His history is highly valued on account of the accuracy of its chronology. [2]

The 11th. century although not so brilliant as the preceding, had some writers of more or less note. One of the most celebrated is, Gregory Magisdros, author of a number of letters imparting information on various subjects ; he wrote a poem of 1000 verses which, it is said, was composed in the course of

---

1 Constantinople, 1774.
2 Paris, 1859.

three days, paraphrased portions of the Old and New Testament, and translated several works from the Greek.

Afterward came, Peter Kedatartz, a Patriarch, and author of hymns in honor of the Martyrs and dead heroes.

Annanias Sanahnetzi, who explained the letters of St. Paul according to the commentaries of St. John Chrysostom and St. Ephrem.

Arisdagues Lasdiverdetzi, author [1] of a History of Armenia from 989 to 1071; he dwells particularly on the destruction of Ani by Alp-Arslan in 1064.

Gregory II, Vegayassere, *Friend of the Martyrs,* also a Patriarch; he translated the Martyrology of Armenia from the Syrian and Greek chronicles.

Sissianos, who composed an eulogy or panegyric of the 40 Martyrs of Sebast.

---

[1] Venice, 1844.

The 12th. century is justly regarded as the most brilliant in the history of Armenian literature, because it produced:

Gregory III. Patriarch, and author of hymns highly esteemed in the Armenian Church, and of an infinite number of letters on different subjects.

Nerses Glayetzi, justly surnamed Shenorhali (Gracious) was considered by the Abbots Villefroy and Villotte, one of most eloquent Fathers of the Armenian Church. He composed a poem of four thousand verses, [1] an admirable work, also a sublime elegy [2] of 2090 verses on the capture of Edessa; a history of Armenia in verse, [3] (a youthful production), and many sacred poems on different subjects. The prose works of

1 Venice, 1830.
2 Paris, 1826.
3 Constantinople, 1824, an incorrect edition. - Venice, 1830.

St. Nerses are equally celebrated. His beautiful prayer is universally known, because it has been printed in all languages[1]; his encyclical pastoral letters [2] are greatly admired, and his homilies, lives of the Saints, etc. etc, have attracted considerable attention. Few authors have been more prolific than Nerses Shenorhali, and no ecclesiastical writer is more popular; he is the Fenelon of Armenia.

Doctor Ignatius, author of a highly esteemed commentary on St. Luke, the Evangelist. [3]

Doctor Sarkis, who composed 43 homilies [4] in imitation of St. Basil, St. Gregory of Nazianze, and particularly that in the style of St. John Chrysostom.

1 Venice, 1862, in 33 languages.
2 St. Petersburg, 1788. - Constantinople, 1821. - Venice, with a latin translation, 1829.
3 Constantinople, 1735, 1824; incorrect.
4 Constantinople, 1743.

John the Deacon, a man of profound erudition, who compiled a detailed chronology that has unfortunately been nearly destroyed; a national history no longer extant, several prayers, beautiful hymns and homilies on different subjects. [1]

Matthew of Edessa, author of a History of his native city from 952 to 1132, a very correct account, which contains many facts relative to the Romans, Persians and Greeks. This history was continued to 1176 by Gregory Yeretz, a disciple of Matthew. These historians give many exact details respecting the Crusades. [2]

Samuel Yeretz, compiled a universal [3] chronology, from the commencement of the World down to 1179; a work highly appreciated.

[1] Venice, 1853.
[2] M. Dulaurier, a distinguished Armenist, has published a French translation at Paris.
[3] Milan, latin translation, 1817.

Mekhithar, a Physician, who is especially renowned as the author of a treatise on Fevers;[1] his work was an embodiment of the ideas or doctrines of the ancient Greek, Persian and Arabian Physicians.

Gregory IV successor and nephew of Nerses Shenorhali, is the author of many letters celebrated for purity and elegance of composition; one of the most admired, is that to the Emperor Comnenus, announcing the death of St. Nerses, and others refer to a proposed re-union of the Greek and Armenian Churches.

Nerses Lampronatzi has composed several works on religious subjects, among which we may mention an admirable discourse,[2] in favor of the union of the Greek and Armenian Churches,

[1] Venice, 1832.
[2] Venice, text with an italian translation, 1812.

which he delivered in a National Council in Romcla in 1179. He is author of two sublime homilies, some letters (one of which is addressed to Leo, King of Armenia) [1], also of many hymns used in the Armenian Church service; he has written and translated several other works.

Mekhithar Kosh is celebrated as the author of ninety fables, [2] which are remarkable for good taste, purity and elegance. Mekhithar also arranged a digest of civil and ecclesiastical Laws, adopting as models the codes of Theodosius and Justinian.

Literature, so flourishing in the 12th. century produced during the 13th. few authors worthy of mention.

Gregory Sguevratzi composed a biographical sketch and eulogy of Nerses

---

[1] Venice, 1787, 1838.
[2] Venice, 1791, 1842, 1854.

Lampronatzi,[1] also homilies, hymns etc. etc.

Mekhithar Anetzi wrote a history of Armenia, Georgia and Persia.

Arisdagues, the Grammarian, is the author of a book entitled "Precepts or directions for learning to write correctly,,, he also compiled a small dictionary of the Armenian language.

John Vanagan termed "the Cenobite,,, was one of the most celebrated writers of this age; he wrote a commentary on Job, and explanations of certain hymns. It is to be regretted, that his History of the Tartar invasion in 1236, is no longer extant.

Vartan, surnamed "The Great,,, was a learned man who understood the Greek, Persian, Hebrew and Tartar languages, and wrote a Universal History from the beginning of the World

---

1 Venice, 1854.

down to 1267, a work of great erudition and very exact in detail [1]; he also composed commentaries on the Holy Scriptures, and wrote several ascetic works. Vartan left 144 fables, which have been re-printed in various places. Forty five of these fables translated by Mr. St. Martin, were published in Paris in 1825.

Doctor Guiragos Kantzaguetzi composed an epitome of Armenian history from the time of King Dertad to the reign of Ayton I., that is to say, from A. D. 300 to 1260. This work contains much desirable informations respecting the Arabs and Tartars [2].

Malachia, the Monk, wrote an interesting account of the irruption of the Tartars, especially of their invasion of Armenia in 1272.

Vahram Rapoun, or "Master,,. Se-

---

1 Moscow, 1861. - Venice, 1862.
2 Venice and Moscow, 1863.

cretary of King Leo III of Armenia, continued in verse the chronicle of Nerses Shenorhali, viz., a rhymed chronology of the Armenian Kings who had reigned in Cylicia [1] until 1280.

John Erzengatzi, the last of the ancient Doctors of the Armenian Church, and of the classic authors of that time, wrote a Key to the Armenian Grammar, a treatise [2] on Astronomy, panegyrics on St. Gregory, [3] a book of prayers, a commentary on the Gospel of St. Matthew, and many songs, hymns, etc.

Stephen Orbelian, [4] Archbishop of Sunik, was the author of a History of his native province. We must here state that M^{r.} St. Martin was laboring under a mistake when he called the "*History of the Orbelians,,* that ac-

1 Madras, 1810.
2 Nakhitchevan in Russia, 1791.
3 Constantinople, 1737, 1824. - Venice 1853.
4 Paris, 1859, - Moscow, 1861.

count of the Georgians which was published at Madras in 1776; it is only a portion of the Stephen's history of Sunik.

Gregory VII Anavarzetzi, Patriarch at Romcla, afterward at Sis; arranged a Calendar according to the Latin standard, and wrote also an Armenian Martyrology, etc. etc.

During the 14th. century, rival factions, termed respectively "The United Brethren,, and "Followers of Datevatzi,,, contributed equally to the corruption of the Armenian language; nevertheless, among the mass of writers a few merit some regard as;

Aïton, (relative and contemporary of King Aïton II), who became a Monk and retired to Cyprus, where he wrote in French, a marvellous History [1] of

---

[1] Venice, 1842, armenian translation with an interesting chronological table by the same author.

the Great Khan, in which he recounts the numerous victories of the Tartars. He also chronicled some of the exploits of the Armenian Kings in Cylicia, (the wars of the Syrians, etc.), and ¦gave interesting details respecting the principal countries of Asia.

Khatchadour Guetcharatzi, a mediocre poet, composed verses and eulogies of Alexander the Great.

Still more unfortunate than the preceding century, the 15th. produced few writers worthy of notice.

Thomas Medzopetzi, wrote a very incorrect history of Tamerlane, and appended to it a chronicle of events which occurred from the time of that great Tartar Prince down to A. D. 1447.

Amirdolvat, a distinguished Physician, left a treatise on the medical art in general.

Literary taste continued for a time to degenerate, yet the 16th. century is remarkable as a new era in letters, for a printing establishment was opened in Venice in 1565, and another press put in operation at Rome in 1584.

Although literature still suffered from the depressing influences of the two preceding centuries, means of general instruction were multiplied. In 1623 the College of the Propaganda organized at Rome, and schools were opened in Etchmiadzin, in Persian Armenia and in Leopol or Lemberg, in Poland, in 1655.

In addition to the printing establishments of Rome and Venice, presses were placed in operation at Leopol in 1616, at Milan in 1624, at Paris in 1633, at Julpha (Tciougha) a suburb of Ispahan, in 1640; at Livorno in 1640; at Amsterdam in 1660; at Marseilles in 1673; at Constantinople in 1677; in Leipsic in 1680; and at Padua in 1690.

The most celebrated of all these

publishing houses was that which was established in Holland.

Among the writers of the 17th. century we may mention, James IV a Patriarch of Armenia.

Stephen of Poland, who translated from Latin into the Armenian language the works of Denis the Areopagite, the History of the Jews by Josephus, and wrote a metaphysical work.

Arakel, who wrote a History [1] of his time, extending from 1601 - 1662.

Bishop Osgan, sent to Holland and afterward to Marseilles to superintend the Armenian printing establishments, edited among other works the Bible.

Matthew Vanantetzi, was the fellow-laborer of Osgan. He established a press in Holland which produced a great many Armenian works.

Another Stephen of Poland, (called Roshkan), compiled a voluminous Dic-

---

[1] Amsterdam, 1669.

tionary of the Armenian - Latin languages.

Gomidas a Martyr at Constantinople in 1707, composed several works, among others, a rhymed chronology of the Greek, Armenian and Persian nations; his brother Eremia has left some annals and historical fragments.

It is true that printing gave a new impulse to Literature, but for a time it served only for the publication of works of little utility. It was reserved for Mekhithar to leave to his Nation disciples well prepared to instruct them, and to bequeath also a rich legacy of precious works, the chief of which is a magnificent Bible, [1] adorned with rare engravings which are now highly appreciated in the East. Mekhithar wrote also an explanation of the Gospel of St. Matthew, [2] and published a Grammar

---

1 Venice, 1733.
2 Venice, 1737.

and an unabridged Dictionary [1] of the Armenian language.

The 18th. century was illustrated by a number of writers, among whom we may cite,

Malachi Diratzou, who wrote chronicles adding to them those of his own time.

James Nalian, Patriarch of Constantinople, author of several works.

Athanasius Merasian, a Bishop, author of a Grammar [2] in three languages, Italian - Armenian - Turkish.

Having passed in review the ancient literature of Armenia, we must now mention the literary impulse of the 18th. century, which so signally preserved and disseminated those treasures of art and science, which the genius of the ancient Armenians had conceived and fostered for thirteen centuries. The honor of this achievement is due to Me-

[1] Venice, 1749.
[2] Venice, 1774.

khithar of Sebaste, the founder of the monastic order which bears his name, and to the co-operation of the disciples whom he educated. This great man's life was consecrated to study, and he succeeded in inspiring his community with a taste for the exact sciences. It is to the Armenian literature thus improved, the establishment of printing presses, and the circulation of books in the national idiom throughout Asia and Europe, that the improvement and progression of the descendants of Haïg are due.

After the Bible and works on religion and the useful arts had been extensively circulated, the Mekhitharist Congregation deemed it incumbent on them to prepare a History of Armenia, and this work was intrusted to Michael Tchamitch, a man of deep and varied acquirements, who was also richly endowed with noble sentiments. He accomplished the task successfully, in three quarto-volumes, giving to the World a complete history of Armenia and its connection with neighbouring countries.

The works of Luke Indjidji on the antiquities and geography of Armenia form a sequel to the valuable history of Tchamitch. These two works are so highly appreciated that they have been translated into the languages of Western Europe. The History by Tchamitch has been published in English; "the Antiquities of Armenia,, in Italian, and the Geography of Indjidji has been translated into German.

Many members of the Mekhitharist Community are conspicuous for talent and erudition, but as want of space precludes the possibility of alluding to all, we will mention only the names and works of Aconce Köver, the biographer of Mekhithar, and an able Geographer; Avedikian, a grammarian and celebrated theologian; Tchaktchak a distinguished lexicographer; the brothers G. and E. Hurmuz, translators and celebrated poets; Aiwazowski, Seth, and Alishan, geographers, historians, and philologists of great merit; Zohrab and Aucher, translators of the chronicles of Eusebius, and R. Trenz a distinguished sacred writer and orator. We regret being unable to pay the tribute of merit due to all the Fathers who have contributed to the honor and glory of the Monastery of St. Lazarus.

Not content with having preserved and enriched the Armenian literature with carefully revived editions of national works, the Mekhitharists have made faithful translations not only of religious and useful books, but of even the literary chefs - d'oeuvre of other nations, and have published in the Armenian language,

Ancient History of Rome, by Rollin.

Treatise on Universal History, by Bossuet. *Funeral Orations*, by the same. *The adventures of Telemachus, Lives of the Philosophers, The education of daughters and The Maxims,* by Fenelon. *The customs of the Israelites and Christians, a Historical catechism,* by Fleury. *The death of Abel,* by Gessner. *An epitome of Roman History* by Goldsmith. *The journey of young Anacharsis in Greece,* by Barthelemew. *Numa Pompilius,* by Florian. *Bellisarius,* by Madame de Genlis. *The solitary Sage or Hermit,* by Pey. *Logic,* by Soave. *Paradise Lost,* by Milton. *Christiade,* Vida. *Night Thoughts,* Young. *Natural History of Birds,* Buffon. *Poems,* Byron. *Life of Julius Cesar,* by Napoleon III, etc.

Among the translations of the works of ancient writers we find, *The Iliad and Odyssy,* Homer. *Tragedies,* Sophocles. *The complete works* of Virgil. *The Poetic Art*, Horace. *Orations,*

Cicero. *Civil Wars and Commentaries, Invasion of Gaul and Britain*, Julius Ceasar. *Philosophical Treatises*, Seneca. *Lives of Illustrious Men*, Plutarch. *Characters*, Theophraste. *Pastoral Laws*, St. Gregory. Also *Select Homilies* by St. Chrysostom and many of the writings of St Augustine.

Among the original works of the community of St. Lazarus, we value highly, the commentaries on the *Old* and *New Testaments; on the Psalms, Ecclesiastics, the Gospel of St. Matthew, and the Epistles of St. Paul*. We would also call attention to their educational works, viz. : — A Universal Biography. A Universal History. The Universal History of the 18th. century ; History of France; History of the Russian Empire ; complete treatises on Rhetoric, Arithmetic, Geometry, Trigonometry, Navigation, as well as on mechanical, liniar and perspective drawing, on ornamental and simple writing, book-keeping, etc. etc. Also works on Medicine, Physiology, Technology, Philosophy, Jurisprudence and Geography.

One of their Geographical works consists of 12 volumes. Another Universal Geography is interspersed with Maps and vignettes, and details much information respecting Armenia which has been collected from the works of ancient writers and modern travellers. An Atlas, copied from the best modern works of the kind, with an introduction on physical and political geography. Academic Dictionary of the Armenian language in two folio volumes, where all the words are verified by quotations from classic authors, and accompanied by Greek and Latin synonyms. - An Armenian Grammar of Grammars or Key to the language, a work of profound learning on a new plan, which cost the author, Father Arsenius Pacradouni,

40 years of study and research. To this learned Father we owe a new poetic metre which he invented and used in his admirable translations of "The Poetic Art,, of Horace, "The Georgics,, of Virgil and Milton's " Paradise Lost. ,, The Armenian nation is also justly proud of the grand epic poem of Father Arsenius Pacradouni called "Haig. ,,

Among the numerous works printed in the Monastery of St. Lazarus is a collection of articles on Moral and Natural sciences, treatises on political economy and general literature.

The poetic works of the Mekhitharist Fathers are printed in three volumes. Monseigneur E. Hurmuz has made a most excellent translation of the Eneid and Eglogues, and a beautiful poem of "The Gardens,, in four cantos.

Many of the literary productions of the Mekhitharist Community prove as useful to the Europeans as to the Armenians, viz.: Grammars, - a French - Armenian, by Father Arsenius Pacradouni; — an Italian - Turkish, by Father Gabriel Avedikian; — English - Armenian, Armenian - English, by Father Pascal Aucher; one Russian - Armenian, by Father Minas Medici; and a German - Armenian, by M. Hindoghlou. There is also a polyglot Grammar, containing the rules or principles of the Turkish, Persian, Arabic and Tartar languages, by Father Minas Medici, a work of great renown, for which the author received a gold medal from the Emperor Nicolas I of Russia.

The Dictionaries are, Armenian - English, English - Armenian, by Father Pascal Aucher; — Italian - Turkish and Armenian - Italian, by Father Emanuel Tchaktchak: - French-Armenian and Armenian-French, by Fath. Pascal Aucher.

A signal service was rendered the literati of all countries, by the publication of the chronicle of Eusebius, (very incomplete in the Greek text), which was translated by the learned Father John Baptist Aucher. Those of Philon, St. Ephraim and Severien are also generally appreciated.

An invaluable work, (especially for foreigners), is the "Quadro della Letteratura Armena,, (Picture of Armenian literature), composed by Monseigneur Sukias de Somal; it gives a correct idea of the progress of Armenian literature from age to age.

While it is true that the Mekhitharist Community gave the first impulse to Armenian literature, it has not been unassisted in its efforts to disseminate the national writings. Credit is also due to other Armenians, who, in imitation of the Monks of St. Lazarus, have propagated their idiom by the publication of various useful works, ancient and modern. The Mekhitharist Community of Vienna have published Histories, written by Caterdjian and Tchakedjian; at Moscow Messrs. J. B. Emine and Osgan have published editions of the works of John Catholicos, Moses of Gaghangadouk, Mekhithar of Aïrivank, Vartan, Guiragos, Stephen Orbelian and Sempad. At Paris M. Chahnazarian brought out the unedited works of several Armenian historians, viz. — Leonce, Stephen Assolig, Vahram Rapoun, Thomas of Medzop and others. At Constantinople Armenian patriots have published the works of Thomas Ardzrouni and Sebeos. There is a large collection of Armenian MSS. at Etchmiadzin, yet the Monks of this patriarchal Monastery have produced very little; we can mention only two works, published by Chahkhatounoff and Djalal on the antiquities of Armenia.

The Armenians resident in India publish works from time to time in Calcutta; those of Georgia do the same at Tiflis.

For several years past the Armenian press in the Monastery of "St. James„ at Jerusalem, has produced little of any importance. (A History of the Armenian Church, was published in 1872.)

A literature as rich as that of Armenia, comprising, as it does, a list of forty historians, exclusive of scientific, theological and grammatical works, could not fail to attract the attention of European Savants. The valuable information that Historians have imparted to us, not only respecting Armenia but the neighbouring nations, has naturally interested the Western people, and, during the present century, the Armenian language has been studied considerably in Europe. Even prior to this epoch Western Savants had translated religious works, and compiled Dictionaries and Grammars of the Armenian tongue. The first Armenian scholar who merits consideration is Barthélemy of Bologna, who lived in the 14th. century. After him came Francis Rivola of Milan in the 17th. Then Clement Galanus, (who composed the *Conciliatio Ecclesiae Armenae cum Romana;*) James Villotte, (a Frenchman). Andreas Accolouth (Prussian), Aug. Pfeiffer (Saxon), Mathurin de la Croze and Villefroy-Abbot of Blamont (both Frenchmen); Schröder, (German). The brothers Whiston, (English) first translators of Moses of Chorene; and of late years, Wahl, Bellaud, St. Martin and the illustrious Lord Byron.

The Savant who has probably given the greatest impulse to Armenian literature in Europe, is St. Martin, a member of the French Institute or Academy, and the author of works on Armenian history and geography, that are justly considered master - pieces of their kind. Unfortunately for Oriental literature, the premature death of St. Martin prevented the accomplishment of his designs.

Among the most celebrated Orientalists of the present day, who are ardently devoted to the study of Armenian literature, we may mention the State Councillor M. Brosset; (a member of the Academy of Science in Russia.) Boettlicher; Boré; the Abbot Cappelletti; Goshe; Neumann and Dulaurier.

The attention of Europe has been particularly attracted to Armenia and its inhabitants by the exploration and narratives of scientists and travellers in the Orient. In addition to the interesting account given by Chardin, de Tournefort, de Jaubert and Klaproth, other travellers have brought to public notice, the heretofore unknown regions where the race of Haïg first established itself. Dubois de Montperreux is the first European who visited in detail and accurately described the region of Great-Armenia. After him Messrs. Texier, Brosset, Abich, Wagner, Khanikoff, and the Fathers Nerses and Stephen of St. Lazarus, traversed the regions of the Caucasus and Upper-Armenia, the localities formerly under the sway of the Arsacidae, the Bagratidae and Roupenians. These travellers published extremely interesting accounts of their journies. At present some courageous explorers are visiting the least frequented parts of Armenia, and others are studying the topography of the regions formerly traversed by the Armenian emigrants who settled in Cylicia and were the first Christians whom the Crusaders met when they entered Asia to wrest the Tomb of Christ from the Infidels.

The Editors of this translation deem it their duty, to add a few words in reference to Mr. Victor Langlois, the author of this work, whose premature death is to be deplored as a severe loss to Archaeology. He was not only a distinguished Archaeologist, but a great Armenian Scholar, who has rendered invaluable services to the literary world.

Among his most useful works we may mention, a Journey through Cylicia; a learned treatise on Armenian numismatics; a collection of historical documents relating to the time of the Roupenian dynasty; translation of the Chronology of Michael the Syrian, etc.

In 1868 he commenced with the co-operation of the Mekhitharists, the publication of the Armenian Historians, with some accounts of their works, which have since been issued from the press.

www.ingramcontent.com/pod-product-compliance
Lightning Source LLC
Chambersburg PA
CBHW020144170426
43199CB00010B/875